Original title:
The Road to Enlightenment Is Paved with Snacks

Copyright © 2025 Creative Arts Management OÜ
All rights reserved.

Author: Maxwell Donovan
ISBN HARDBACK: 978-1-80566-019-4
ISBN PAPERBACK: 978-1-80566-314-0

Nibbles of Knowledge

In a world of tasty bites,
Wisdom's hidden throughout the nights.
Chips of clarity, pretzels of thought,
Each munch a lesson, can't be bought.

Crispy crackers, they hold the key,
Peanut butter thoughts flow wild and free.
Each graham's a riddle, wrapped up in fun,
Snack time's the teacher, we've only begun.

Flavors of Freedom

Caramel drips and a dash of glee,
Popcorn wisdom sprinkles the spree.
Each fruity chew brings a newfound view,
With every crunch, we start anew.

Chocolates melt as the mind expands,
Freedom's flavor in our hands.
Savoring life, one bite at a time,
Sweet revelations wrapped in a rhyme.

Snacktime Serenity

Find peace in a bag of cheese puffs,
Munching away all the tough stuff.
Each bite whispers secrets of calm,
Satisfaction in cheesy balm.

Nothing like popcorn to lift the mood,
While nachos dance, oh, what a brood!
Dips of reflection, a side of fun,
In snacktime's embrace, we're all one.

Chews of Change

Biting into freedom with every chip,
Crunching away all restrictions, let it rip!
Each gummy bear a step forward clear,
Sweet little changes that bring us cheer.

Fluffy marshmallows float in fresh air,
Softness embraces, with a hint of dare.
Every treat tells a story of gain,
In each chewing moment, we break the chain.

Savory Wisdom

Snack of life, a crispy chip,
Crumbled thoughts on every trip.
Nibbles vast, both bold and bright,
Salty truths come to light.

In mid-bite, I ponder fate,
Dips of joy on every plate.
The crunch reveals a hidden tale,
Snack and laugh, let humor sail.

Delicious Detours

Munching paths both wide and narrow,
Candy-coated truths do sparrow.
With popcorn clouds, we drift and sway,
Finding bliss along the way.

Chocolate dreams in gooey streams,
Savoring life's delicious schemes.
Pie-in-the-sky, I take a leap,
Snacking's secrets I will keep.

Small Plates, Big Ideas

Tiny bites bring mega thoughts,
Salads, fries, and honeyed knots.
Every morsel holds a clue,
Snack-sized notes for me and you.

Sushi rolls and nacho flights,
Gastronomic, fun-filled nights.
In each dish, a giggling muse,
Bite and ponder, and then we choose.

Enlightened Edibles

With every burger, wisdom flows,
Gravy boats on rivers, who knows?
Fries of joy and cakes of cheer,
Gourmet laughs, oh bring them near!

Mindful munching, snack parade,
Each silly bite, a laugh cascade.
As I crunch, my heart does sing,
Life's true lessons in everything.

Munching on the Mystical

Chips of wisdom crunch so loud,
Sat in meditation, feeling proud.
Pretzel twists of fate align,
With each bite, I sip the divine.

Nibbles of bliss, my spirit lifts,
Chocolate bars are my best gifts.
Crunchy munch, it's not so deep,
In snacks I seek, my soul to keep.

Flavorful Footprints

Walking through life, I skip and hop,
With gummy bears, I never stop.
Each step a flavor, a joyous spree,
In candy roads, I find the key.

Bite-sized lessons on my feet,
Marshmallow clouds, a tasty treat.
Every snack a quirky tale,
In this journey, I never fail.

Sweet Reveries

Dreams of sugar, light as air,
Macaron moons are beyond compare.
Filling my heart with every bite,
Sprinkles of joy, oh what a sight!

Caramel rivers, flowing sweet,
A chocolate sun warms my feet.
In this confectionery dreamland,
Sugar rush, it's simply grand!

Chewy Encounters

Gummy worms wriggle, sharing a laugh,
In a chewy world, we share the path.
Licorice thoughts, so dark and profound,
With every chew, wisdom is found.

Popcorn kernels, light and bright,
In kernels of truth, we find delight.
Snackers unite on this fun ride,
With every munch, let joy be our guide.

Savoring the Pathway to Insight

With chips in hand, we take a stand,
To munch our way through life's demands.
Each crispy crunch ignites a thought,
A snack-filled quest for wisdom sought.

Beneath the stars, we dip and munch,
A revelations served with every crunch.
Cheetos crumbs like sparks of truth,
In the silly game of snack-filled youth.

Bites of Awareness

A donut's glaze, a spark of light,
Each bite reveals new insight.
Twinkies whisper sweet delight,
As wisdom blooms in every bite.

Popcorn kernels, puffed and bright,
Shower thoughts in crispy flight.
With every nibble, we advance,
Toward tasty truths, a merry dance.

The Trail of Taste and Truth

On this trail of tasty bites,
Chocolate bars bring happy nights.
With gummy bears as guides and friends,
The flavor journey never ends.

Pretzels twist like thoughts that bend,
With dips and laughs, we joyfully blend.
Through every snack, the laughs ignite,
Turning crumbs into sheer delight.

Epiphanies Served on Platter

Nachos piled like dreams we chase,
A piquant spice to ease the race.
Each salsa dip, a deep insight,
Served warm and bright, a tasty bite.

With cupcakes crowned like glowing stars,
Our thoughts take flight, we laugh on bars.
A platter full of jest and glee,
Snack-induced truths make us feel free.

Chips of Clarity

In a bag so crisp and bright,
Potato dreams take flight.
Each crunch is wisdom's call,
With every bite, I feel so tall.

Salsa dips and guac galore,
Snack time opens the door.
With every chip I munch today,
I laugh my doubts all away.

Crumbs of Consciousness

On this plate of tiny bites,
Crackers shine with all their lights.
Each nibble brings a thought anew,
Who knew wisdom is baked in too?

Grazing here like grazing cows,
Finding meaning in my brows.
The crumbs I leave, they whisper loud,
In snack-time bliss, I feel so proud.

Treats for the Soul

Chocolate bars and chewy treats,
Lift my spirit, can't be beat.
With each sweet, my worries fade,
Life's mysteries we'll invade.

Gummy bears dance in delight,
Underneath the moonlit night.
Each flavor sings of joy and cheer,
Snack by snack, I persevere.

Edibles of Awareness

Popcorn kernels, fluffy, round,
In their crunch, new thoughts are found.
With melted butter, I can see,
The truth awaits in every spree.

As I munch on every piece,
My fretful mind begins to cease.
The universe in every grain,
A snack attack reveals the sane.

Culinary Clarity

As I munch on fries with glee,
Life's mysteries unfold like a spree.
Each bite a lesson, crisp and clear,
Snack time wisdom, oh so near.

A chocolate bar sparks a thought,
Enlightenment the snack shop bought.
Popcorn pops with ideas that fly,
Salted reflections in the sky.

Crisp Crunches of Consciousness

Chips crunch loud in the quiet night,
As I ponder my snack-filled plight.
Each crinkle of the bag I hear,
Is a voice of wisdom drawing near.

Carrot sticks whisper, stay on course,
While soda bubbles bubble with force.
In this banquet of thought, I dine,
Finding peace in the cheese and vine.

Nourishment for the Soul's Quest

Cookies crumble like old beliefs,
Sweet treats bring joy, not just relief.
With every nibble, I think and chew,
Are snacks the key to know what's true?

Nutty flavors of enlightenment bite,
While cupcakes dance in soft moonlight.
Every slice of pizza's a chance to explore,
In this culinary quest, who could ask for more?

Temptations on the Trail

Granola bars guide my weary feet,
Each munch ignites a tasty beat.
Nuts and raisins, my trusty friends,
Fueling wisdom that never ends.

Lollipops swinging from wisdom trees,
Dancing breezes bring snacks with ease.
Pop tart dreams, colorful and bright,
Leading me to a profound delight.

Snacking on Stillness

In the quiet, munch I do,
Potato chips and thoughts anew.
Crunching softly on my fate,
Waiting for my mind to sate.

Sipping tea with calm delight,
Cookies whisper through the night.
Meditation? I just snack,
Where's my inner peace? Oh, back!

Flavorful Footsteps

Walking slowly, crumbs I shed,
Chocolate-covered dreams I spread.
Each step brings a tasty prize,
Honeyed laughter, sweetened eyes.

Gummy bears lead me away,
To a land of bright parfaits.
Every path's a treat delight,
Savoring both day and night.

Delights of Discovery

Found a donut on the way,
Strawberry glaze, oh what a play!
With each bite, a rumor spreads,
Sugar-coated thoughts in heads.

Behind each mind's a hidden snack,
Caramel thoughts they might not lack.
Peanut butter lifts the mood,
In this feast, I'm feeling good.

Gourmet Growth

I've grown wise on veggies green,
Salsa dancing on the scene.
Every morsel sparks a thought,
In this garden, joy is caught.

Anticipating bites with glee,
Avocado dreams, come sip with me!
Learning life with every taste,
Grateful for this snack-filled haste.

Flavor Journeys Await

With chips alone, I take a trip,
A crunch that makes my spirit flip.
Each flavor joins, a merry crew,
From BBQ to sour blue.

Popcorn kernels, popping bright,
Guide me through the snacktime night.
In every bite, a tale is spun,
Of salty dreams and cheesy fun.

Small Snacks, Grand Insights

A pretzel knot, a twist of fate,
In every nibble, wisdom's weight.
Peanut butter, sticky muse,
Sparks of knowledge, I can't refuse.

Granola bars, in pockets hide,
Sweet surprises, I confide.
Each tiny morsel holds a key,
Unlocking thoughts, oh so free!

In the Kitchen of Consciousness

Sizzling pans, a wondrous space,
Where fries and cookies trade their grace.
Baking cakes, a meditative spree,
Flour dreams dance in harmony.

Stirring chili, a spicy quest,
In every simmer, life's a jest.
Ladle out laughter, flavors collide,
In my mind's kitchen, joy's abide.

Biting into Wisdom

A donut ring, a circle true,
Eating round, my thoughts renew.
Glazed with insights, sweetly spun,
In every bite, a tasty pun.

Bite-sized truths in sushi rolls,
Help uncover life's hidden goals.
With every munch, the world expands,
Nourishment comes in playful hands.

Plates of Peace

In the pantry, dreams collide,
Chips and cookies, side by side.
Searching for truth in every crunch,
Finding wisdom in a munch.

Chocolate bars, oh, what a clue,
Hidden messages in fondue.
Enlightenment's not far away,
With every snack, it's a buffet!

Pretzels twist like life's great maze,
Each dip a moment, lost in haze.
Grabbing goodies, with every bite,
Laughing hard into the night.

With popcorn popping, thoughts take flight,
Floating high, oh what a sight!
Wisdom served on a silver tray,
Snack your way to the light of day.

Savoring Each Step

Bite by bite, the journey goes,
Nibbles yield life's highs and lows.
With gummy bears as guides so sweet,
Every moment tastes like a treat.

Fries for thought, they make me smile,
Each catnap's worth a tasty while.
Hold the salsa, make it bold,
With every chip, life's secrets unfold.

Lemon drops for sour times,
With each legume, a sage that rhymes.
Snack-sorcery in every flavor,
Finding peace, oh what a savor!

So munch away, don't hesitate,
Mysteries wrapped upon your plate.
The fun in snacking brings delight,
As laughter lingers with each bite.

Craving Curiosity

In the depths of my hunger, I seek to explore,
A bag of chips whispers, "There's so much more!"
Crunching through thoughts, I munch on my dreams,
Each flavor a lesson, or so it seems.

Gummy bears giggle, as wisdom takes flight,
Chocolate bars battle in a sweet little fight.
With popcorn philosophies popping in air,
I stumble on answers, sprinkled with care.

Chewing the Cud of Contemplation

Sipping on soup while I ponder the stars,
Each spoonful a question, reaching so far.
Do snacks hold the answers? I chew on my fate,
As a donut suggests, 'You just need to wait!'

Pretzels twist wisdom in salty old rings,
As I dip into thoughts of what munching brings.
With nachos of insight, I snack and I stare,
Should I crunch or should I munch? Life's snack time affair.

Pastries of Perception

Cupcakes of clarity sparkle with cream,
Each bite is a venture, a delicious dream.
I ponder the frosting, a swirl on my mind,
Sugar-coated questions, the answers I find.

Cookies of chaos, crumbled with glee,
Each taste a new vision, life's sweet mystery.
With sprinkles of knowledge that dance on my tongue,
I nibble on thoughts that keep me so young.

Fork in the Road of Fulfillment

Here lies a fork, with snacks on each side,
One leads to veggies, the other to fried.
I laugh at the choice, a dilemma for sure,
As brownies beckon boldly, I'm tempted to blur.

Navigating flavors, I wade through the zest,
Each crunch holds a promise, a tasty quest.
So I raise up my snack, in joy I confide,
Life's crispy conundrums, oh how they provide!

Sips of Serenity and Snacks of Insight

Fresh brew in my cup, oh what a delight,
Each sip brings a chuckle, a soft warm light.
As cookies crumble softly, wisdom takes a seat,
Turns out, snacks are the key to thoughts most sweet.

In between the munching, giggles take their flight,
Chips whisper secrets, oh what a funny sight!
With every crunchy bite, we journey to new highs,
Snack time is the best time, it's no surprise.

Bounty of Being.

Life's platter full of chips, each crunch a little cheer,
Peanut butter dreams dance, bringing friends quite near.
Popcorn thoughts are popping, like kernels in the fire,
In the bounty of this moment, we find what we desire.

Hands in the cookie jar, laughter fills the air,
With every tasty morsel, wisdom sits to share.
This banquet of delights leads us on a quest,
For snacks and silly moments, truly are the best.

Pathways of Whimsy

Lollipops and laughter, paths turn sweet and round,
Chocolate-covered giggles spill from every mound.
Every gummy bear brings a grin that's hard to hide,
On this path of whimsy, the heart feels open wide.

Pretzels twist like riddles, laughter twirls anew,
With every crunch and munch, there's so much we can do.
Popcorn kernels dance, popping wisdom here and there,
In this playful journey, we find joy everywhere.

Morsels of Mindfulness

Peanut brittle wisdom wrapped in sugary delight,
Each bite brings clarity, from morning until night.
Fruit loops of insight roll 'round a colorful bowl,
In munching on these morsels, we nourish heart and soul.

Crackers stacked with laughter, a tower oh so tall,
As we nibble and chuckle, we feel we're having a ball.
The snackable reflections, so playful and so bright,
In every tasty moment, we find our inner light.

Bites of the Beyond

In the pantry, treasures hide,
Crunchy crisps, our hearts' delight.
Each munch unfolds a side,
Snickers spark a joyful flight.

Chocolate rivers flow in dreams,
Popcorn clouds burst with squeals.
Every nibble, or so it seems,
Brings us closer to the feels.

Satisfying the Soul

A cookie whispers sweetly now,
With frosting smiles, don't ask me how.
Each bite's a hug on paws and claws,
Elevating munching to applause.

Chips crunch loud, a joyous cheer,
As salsa swirls unaware of fear.
Popcorn kernels dance around,
In this feast, pure joy is found.

Munchies of Mindful Moments

Gummy bears wander through the mind,
In chewy quests, truth we find.
Each flavor tells a story bright,
As we snack into the night.

Carrot sticks on wisdom's trail,
Dip them well, don't let them fail.
Sweet and savory, life's a game,
Each crunch adds to our fame.

Taste Test for Transformation

Fried delights in golden wraps,
Transforming frowns into high claps.
With each spoonful and every swirl,
Our inner munchkin starts to twirl.

Doughnuts sprinkled, laughter's mix,
Syrupy bliss, a clever fix.
As we feast, the world feels light,
Snack on, friends, into the night!

Palette of Perception

From chips of wisdom, we munch away,
Each dip a lesson, each crunch a play.
With flavors that tickle the curious mind,
We savor the journey, unconfined.

A sprinkle of humor, a dash of zest,
Our thoughts dance lightly, never at rest.
As we nibble on truth, our spirits lift,
With every bite taken, we find our gift.

Gastronomic Growth

In a banquet of books, we feast with glee,
Each chapter a flavor, a taste to see.
With popcorn ideas popping all around,
We munch through tales, where wisdom is found.

A cupcake of kindness, a cookie of joy,
Nourishing thoughts, nothing to destroy.
Bite-sized insights, served on a plate,
With every morsel, we celebrate fate.

Crunching Concepts

With every crunch, we ponder and chew,
Layered thoughts sprout; they blossom anew.
Like nachos with cheese, messy yet bright,
Ideas cascade in a flavorful flight.

A taco of laughter, a wrap of delight,
Together we snack as we share insights.
Between bites of nonsense, we find some grace,
In this silly buffet, we embrace the chase.

Gratifying Grains

Oats of knowledge, wholesome and true,
With a sprinkle of humor, the mind will break through.
We sip on some soup, contemplating the day,
A savory journey, in a fun-loving way.

Rice cakes of reason, light and so airy,
We munch through absurdity, never too scary.
With each bite we take, we laugh and we learn,
In this tasty adventure, for wisdom we yearn.

Journey to Inner Bliss

In a land where cupcakes glow,
Wisdom's served with nachos, yo.
I sip my drink, a fizzy cheer,
The path ahead is bright and clear.

With pretzels shaping thoughts so fine,
Each bite's a treat, a tasty sign.
Enlightenment, a tasty quest,
With gummy bears, I feel the best.

I stumble on a chocolate brook,
In this sweet land, I can't help but look.
Beneath the stars, I find my way,
With candy clouds that dance and sway.

Munching Through the Maze of Wisdom

Through tunnels of popcorn, I weave,
In this maze, I shall not grieve.
With candy canes as my guide,
Every snack is a joyful ride.

Sipping soda, I take a leap,
In this sweet world, secrets keep.
A donut here, a cookie there,
Each bite whispers without a care.

Navigating chips and dips,
Each crunch reveals the best of tips.
In chocolate rivers, I find my clue,
Munching my way to something new.

Crumbs of Cosmic Clarity

Amidst the chips, I ponder deep,
In cookie crumbles, wisdom's steep.
A sprinkle here, a frosting there,
Sweet revelations fill the air.

Beneath the stars, I eat my pie,
With each slice, the truths comply.
Jelly beans paint the night so bright,
Bringing clarity with every bite.

In every bite, a lesson found,
With candy wisdom, I'm spellbound.
As marshmallows float in cosmic dance,
I munch my way into a trance.

Nibbles of New Perspectives

With every nibble, I explore,
New flavors waiting to adore.
Gummy worms teach me to sway,
As I redefine my day.

A light-hearted snack sets me free,
Custard cups invite the glee.
In every crunch, fresh thoughts arise,
As I feast beneath the skies.

In chocolate sprinkles, wisdom lies,
With every bite, the world complies.
Through laughter, joy, and blissful eats,
I munch my way through life's sweet feats.

Flaky Lessons

Beneath the layers, secrets hide,
A croissant whispers, 'Come inside.'
But donuts call with sugary glee,
As I stumble towards pastry mastery.

Crumbs on my shirt, wisdom's delight,
Each flake a lesson, oh what a sight!
With chocolate sprinkles, I ponder fate,
Is this enlightenment or just my plate?

Bakers bake, and I just snack,
Kneading dough, I lose my track.
Each nibble leads to curious thought,
Are snacks the answers? Or just what I sought?

Funny how fruit tart can reveal,
The zest of life is what we feel.
In every crunch, the truth will show,
Enlightenment's sweet—let the muffin flow!

Tasty Trials

In the kitchen, I start to mix,
A pinch of joy and a dash of tricks.
Flour flies with a wink and a grin,
Oh, how to find where enlightenment's been?

I batter my woes with icing bright,
Chocolates melt in warm delight.
With a sprinkle of courage, and a dash of flair,
My trials turn tasty—oh, what a pair!

Every nibble is a step anew,
Learning to savor each bite so true.
A cookie crumbles under the stress,
But with milk on hand, I find success.

Through trials of sweet, I'll never fret,
For in every snack, a lesson's set.
With giggles and crumbs, life's joy takes flight,
In this tasty journey, I'll find the light!

Bliss in Every Bite

A slice of cake, oh what a dream,
Each mouthful bursts like a sunbeam.
Frosting flows like wisdom sweet,
In sugary bites, life's joys compete.

When pizza calls, I take my stand,
A cheesy slice in my eager hand.
Crusty edges whisper so clear,
With every bite, I conquer fear.

Oh, the joy of salty and sweet,
In every morsel, life feels complete.
So I laugh with each cheesy grin,
For bliss in snacks, we all can win!

Nibbling slowly, I ponder fate,
Is bliss just a snack on a paper plate?
With giggles and grins, I take the chance,
To munch my way through this cosmic dance!

Sweets of Self-Exploration

With gummy bears, I find my way,
Exploring life in a chewy play.
Licorice roads twist and turn,
In every bite, I crave to learn.

Chocolate rivers flow so deep,
In molten swirls, mysteries creep.
Each jelly bean, a choice so bold,
In flavor adventures, stories unfold.

A sprinkle of nuts, a hint of spice,
Discovering joy—oh, isn't it nice?
With every crunch, I redefine,
The snacks of wisdom, which are all mine.

So grab your snacks and join the ride,
For in every flavor, there's truth to guide.
With laughter and crumbs, let's taste and find,
Sweets of self, oh, they're one of a kind!

Snacks of Serenity

In a world of chips and dips,
Peace comes in crunchy bits.
Tacos whisper sweet delight,
Guiding souls through starry night.

Chocolate bars, a quiet treat,
Melt away the stress we meet.
With every bite, a joyful cheer,
Savoring moments, bringing near.

Popcorn kernels, light and airy,
In each crunch, life feels less scary.
Pretzel knots twisted with glee,
Unlocking laughter, wild and free.

Granola bites, a crunchy cue,
Showing us what peace can do.
Embrace the munch, let worries wane,
In every nibble, lose the pain.

Gastronomic Glimpses of Grace

While seeking truths in every bite,
Pizza spins with cheesy light.
Joy spreads like butter on toast,
Finding flavors, we love most.

Carrots crunch with laughter's flare,
Celery sticks, a veggie dare.
Even cake can teach us zen,
Bringing smiles again and again.

Crispy nachos, a spicy flair,
Each chip says, "Hey, please come share!"
With guacamole, humor tries,
Beneath the sun, our spirits rise.

Doughnuts ring with sugary bliss,
In each bite, we find our wish.
Life's a buffet, come take a taste,
In every treat, the joy's not waste.

Chewy Choices on the Journey

On this path of chewy snacks,
Gummis bounce with playful acts.
Licorice ropes we follow tight,
Tugging at our hearts, pure light.

Granola bars with crunchy hugs,
Bite-sized joy, not just for bugs.
Pudding cups, oh soft and sweet,
Life's mysteries in every treat.

Nutty clusters dance and sing,
Whispering secrets of the spring.
With every chew, we lose our cares,
Finding wisdom in what we share.

Cheeseballs roll, a jolly crew,
Laughter binds like gooey glue.
Snack away, our spirits soar,
In every moment, we explore.

Tasting the Infinite

In every nibble, worlds unfold,
Cookies bring tales yet untold.
Chips that crackle with delight,
Feed the soul through day and night.

Ice cream scoops, a creamy dream,
Sweetness flows, a gentle stream.
Fruits of nature, bright and bold,
Savor life, let joy take hold.

Sushi rolls, a twist of fate,
Delicacies to elevate.
In every morsel, laughter's grace,
Tasting joy in every place.

Feast on wisdom, munch on glee,
Every snack, a memory.
With laughter shared and hearts aglow,
The flavor of life continues to grow.

Sips of Spirituality

A cup of tea in hand, I sip,
Divine thoughts swirl, take a dip.
Chai and giggles stir the mind,
In these brews, peace we find.

Cookies crumble, souls delight,
Each nibble brings a twinkling light.
Meditation with a muffin bite,
Snack time leads to inner sight.

Tastes of Truth

A chocolate bar, sweet divine,
Each bite reveals wisdom fine.
With peanut butter, spread it wide,
Truth sticks to thoughts like a joyful glide.

Chips that crunch as laughter soars,
Sound of happiness, open doors.
Taste the joy, let worries cease,
These savory snacks bring inner peace.

Culinary Contemplation

Pretzels twisted, thoughts unbent,
In every flavor, wisdom's sent.
Savoring crumbs from lofty goals,
Fried delights, feeding the souls.

Nachos piled, a sight to see,
Dip into life with pure glee.
Salsa dances, dreams ignite,
Crunchy snacks spark divine insight.

Savory Steps to Illumination

Popcorn pops, ideas bloom,
In the theater of the room.
Each kernel's burst, a thought's delight,
Crisp revelations come to light.

A donut's ring, a circle's truth,
Sweet sprinkles of joyful youth.
In every bite, wisdom's flash,
With tasty treats, we make a splash.

Piquant Paths to Presence

A peppered trail I roam,
With every crunch, I find my home.
Chili flakes on chips abide,
In spicy nibbles, joy can't hide.

Salsa dancing on my tongue,
A zesty song that's just begun.
Each bite a burst of tasty cheer,
In savory snacks, my mind is clear.

Crisp cookies whisper tales of fate,
With chocolate drips, they satiate.
I laugh aloud at life's delight,
As sweet and salty sparks take flight.

Each crumby step brings laughter near,
A jovial journey, full of cheer.
In every munch and every crunch,
I find my bliss in snacky lunch.

Sweet Revelations along the Way

In candies bright, I seek the truth,
A gummy bear provides sweet proof.
With every chew, a lesson learned,
In sugary bites, my worries burned.

Marshmallow clouds float overhead,
While chocolates dance, my hunger fed.
Just like the sweets, life's twists unfold,
With sticky moments, stories told.

A sprinkle here, a drizzle there,
Each sugary path, I do declare.
In laughter shared, we find our light,
With frosting dreams, the world feels right.

From lollipops to taffy strings,
Who knew that joy could come from things?
Each treat a spark, a little cheer,
In sugar worlds, I hold so dear.

Morsels of Mindfulness

A tiny crunch, a world so vast,
With every nibble, I hold fast.
In mindful bites, I learn to pause,
Each snack becomes a worthy cause.

Popcorn pops, thoughts fly away,
As kernels dance, I start to play.
With butter drizzles, I explore,
My mind expands with every score.

A piece of chocolate melts my frown,
In squares of joy, I wear my crown.
With every morsel, wisdom stores,
In crunchy layers, life restores.

So come, let's snack and elevate,
Through crispy treats, we resonate.
In every bite, the now I heed,
With playful snacks, my soul is freed.

Flavorful Fables of the Soul

In tangy tales, the flavors blend,
With cheesy bites, I start to mend.
A nacho chip, a fable's root,
In crunchy layers, wisdom's fruit.

As hot wings soar on wings of spice,
I chase the thrill, oh, isn't it nice?
With every dip, a story spins,
In tasty bites, my joy begins.

A cookie's crunch, a classic twist,
In sweet delight, I can't resist.
With tales of flavor, life's a feast,
In snacking moments, worry ceased.

So gather 'round this hearty spread,
With snacks that dance inside my head.
In flavorful fables, laughter swirls,
As every bite unfurls new worlds.

Appetizers of Awareness

Small bites bring big thoughts,
Munching while we ponder,
Chips of wisdom in a bowl,
Popcorn musings, we wander.

Dips of insight on the side,
Celery sticks, so bright and green,
With every crunch, we glide,
Contemplating the unseen.

From veggie trays to cheese-filled dreams,
A plate of laughter waits for all,
Nibbling on life's silly themes,
We stumble but never fall.

As we snack, we find our way,
With donuts swirling thoughts anew,
Each flavor serves to brightly play,
Exploring life with every chew.

Crunchy Connections

Crisp bites echo with delight,
Chili fries and nachos cheer,
In this crunchy, tasty night,
All our worries disappear.

Pretzel knots and popcorn bites,
Each texture tells a funny tale,
With laughter reaching dizzy heights,
Cheese puns never seem to fail.

Nibbles shared in joyful haste,
Connecting souls one chip at a time,
With every dip, we savor taste,
As laughter flows, so does the rhyme.

In the midst of cheesy bliss,
We find a path through gooey fun,
Snack by snack, we cannot miss,
This journey only just begun.

Piquant Paths

Spicy bites ignite the quest,
Salsa dancing on a spoon,
Hot sauce leaps from sweet to zest,
Chili dreams beneath the moon.

Savory treats, a misfit crew,
Crispy wings, a friendship spark,
With jalapeños breaking through,
We laugh until the night gets dark.

Onion rings and garlic bread,
Each crunch leads us near and far,
While munching, wisdom's often bred,
With fries to guide, we set the bar.

Laughter flares as snacks align,
Exploring flavors, bold and bright,
Through piquant paths, we intertwine,
With laughter bringing us delight.

Zesty Zen

Citrus bursts, a sunny cheer,
Lemonade and ginger snacks,
Every sip quenches a fear,
As we gather, spirits relax.

Fruity bites, the sweetest scenes,
Bananas, berries, all in line,
Finding joy in little beans,
Snacking makes our thoughts align.

With each morsel, mellow vibes,
Zucchini slices, crispy, fine,
Discussion flows, our laughter tribes,
As snacks evict the daily grind.

In this zestful, merry dance,
Our hearts unite in crunchy cheer,
Hand in hand, we take a chance,
For snack-filled joy is always near.

Blissful Bites

In the land of crunch and munch,
Wisdom came in every lunch.
A cookie here, a chip so bold,
Snack time tales that never get old.

With every crunch, a giggle shared,
Life's little lessons, brightly aired.
Choco bars and funny pies,
Unlocking truth behind each guise.

Tasty treats became so wise,
In crispy crunch, no room for lies.
Popcorn thoughts that flew so high,
While gummy bears taught me to fly.

So munch away, don't miss the chance,
For every nibble sparks a dance.
In every bite, a smile ignites,
Snack your way to deeper sights.

Golden Grahams of Growth

Marshmallow dreams and graham delight,
Teach me lessons wrapped up tight.
With every crunch, a new idea,
S'mores of wisdom draw me near.

Nibbling time, a toast to me,
Each bite reveals what's meant to be.
Honey drips of golden fate,
Sweetened bites that can't wait.

Tiny nuggets of truth abound,
In crunchy comfort, growth is found.
So grab a bowl, dig in with cheer,
Life's tasty snacks, forever near.

With every spoonful, joy expands,
Each grain of wisdom in our hands.
Let's savor growth with every taste,
Golden bites that never waste.

Regal Recipes for Reflection

A pinch of salt, and laughter's spice,
Stirring thoughts won't break the dice.
Whisking dreams with berries bright,
Feasting in the soft moonlight.

Broccoli crowns of regal flair,
Dancing hats in evening air.
Sipping soup of sage delight,
Every gulp a giggling flight.

From careful hands to trusty pots,
Cooking up the best of thoughts.
Seasoned wisdom in each bite,
Nibbles that make spirits light.

Serve reflections on a plate,
A tasty truth to celebrate.
With every dish, a smile ignites,
In cooking's joy, we find new sights.

Platefuls of Perspective

A plate of hues, a splash of flair,
Each food tells a story rare.
Carrot sticks with funky dips,
Life's lessons in salty chips.

Gather 'round for tasty talks,
Sharing truths in savory walks.
Fries of wisdom, hot and crisp,
Flavors dance, they curl and lisp.

In apple pie, reflections swell,
With every slice, the stories tell.
Hold the bowl and take a bite,
Life's banquet of sheer delight.

So venture forth with plates in hand,
Snack your way through this wild land.
For every munch, a giggle grows,
In every bite, the wisdom flows.

Culinary Clarity

In the kitchen, chaos reigns,
Chips and dips like knowledge gained.
Every bite a spark of light,
Satisfying every appetite.

Chocolate bars can clear the haze,
In sugary bliss, the mind will blaze.
With every crunch, a thought takes flight,
Snack away, it feels so right.

Carrots and celery, not as fun,
Where's the laughter? Where's the pun?
Snack on joy, let troubles cease,
In every nibble, find your peace.

So grab a treat, don't overthink,
Every crunch brings wisdom, I think.
Serve up smiles in playful heaps,
Grab your snacks, and take the leaps!

Delicacies of Desire

Fried pickles call, a siren's tune,
A savory dance beneath the moon.
Each crisp embrace, a sweet romance,
As we revel in each bite's chance.

Gummy bears, oh, how they cheer,
Chewing joy with every tear.
Sprinkled candies light the way,
To munch away the doubts of day.

Cheesecake bites adorned with flair,
Turning frowns into laughter's air.
With each slice, we'll spread delight,
In every morsel, hearts ignite.

So gather 'round with snacks to share,
Life's finest gifts are everywhere.
In sweet indulgence, dreams conspire,
For when we snack, we reach much higher!

Morsels of the Mind

Crunchy wisdom in every chip,
Dip your worries, take a trip.
In pretzel twists our thoughts unwind,
Salty snacks and peace aligned.

Cookies crumble, thoughts unfold,
In chocolate dreams, there's wisdom sold.
Bite after bite, a noodle's tale,
A pasta path, we shall not fail.

Peanut butter spreads are deep,
On toast of knowledge, take a leap.
With flavor bursting, find your way,
Snack your troubles far away.

So let us feast on joy and cheer,
With every snack, our minds are clear.
Morsels guide us through the haze,
In funny feasts, we sing our praise!

Treats on the Trail

Granola bars as trail snacks call,
Fueling journeys, big and small.
With every cheery crunch we sing,
Adventure waits with every fling.

Popcorn poppin', laughter flies,
Bite-sized journeys greet the skies.
In nugget joy, we find our peace,
As crumbs of fun never cease.

Donuts glazed with dreams so sweet,
Guide our steps with tasty feet.
Snack at noon, or even night,
Like fireflies, we spark delight.

So pack your treats and hold them tight,
With every nibble, life feels right.
On trails of laughter, joy's our goal,
For every snack feeds the soul!

Bites of Bliss

In the pantry, I take a peek,
Happiness hides and seeks.
Chocolate bars, oh what a find,
Nibbles for the curious mind.

Popcorn pops like little stars,
Snacking dreams from near to far.
Potato chips in crunching cheer,
Each bite brings me closer here.

Flavorful Journeys

Trail mix in my trusty pack,
Each nut a step along the track.
Granola bars that gently tease,
Fuel for thoughts that come with ease.

Cookies whisper, 'Stay awhile!',
Their sweet aroma makes me smile.
Jellybeans in colors bright,
Roadside stops bring pure delight.

Delights of Discovery

Savoring bites, I take a chance,
Every morsel, a little dance.
Ice cream cones, a melting sun,
With every scoop, my joy has spun.

Peanut butter, sticky bliss,
Toast and treats, how could I miss?
Friendly snacks in tasty play,
Guide me on my snack-filled way.

Crisp Paths to Insight

Nachos piled with cheesy dreams,
Each chip holds hope, or so it seems.
Veggie sticks dipped in ranchy flow,
Crunchy wisdom in every row.

Muffins rising like bright ideas,
Sourdough hugs, the heart it cheers.
Every bite a nugget shared,
In this feast, no soul is spared.

Edible Wisdom

In a world of sweet delight,
I munch my way through day and night.
Each chip and dip a lesson found,
With every bite, enlightenment's crowned.

Potato puffs and cheese galore,
Each crunch reveals a secret door.
If knowledge comes from every snack,
I'll take the shortcut, never look back.

A cookie crumb, a nugget's gleam,
Nibbles spark the best of dreams.
With candies wrapped in wisdom's guise,
I feast upon my sweet surprise.

From jelly beans to gummy bears,
Snack-sized truth dissolves my cares.
In every bite, a giggle stirs,
Enlightenment? Just pass the spurs!

Whispers of Flavor

The whispers call, a savory tune,
As popcorn pops beneath the moon.
Each kernel bursts with little bling,
In every crunch, enlightenment sings.

A nibble here, a bite right there,
The flavors dance in tasty flair.
Chips that whisper secrets bold,
Of wisdom wrapped in salty gold.

Marshmallow fluff and peanut spread,
Lead me well, as I am fed.
Each flavor blends to form a spell,
In every morsel, stories dwell.

Sorbet smooth, and cake that's light,
Bring forth truths in bites of delight.
With laughter shared and snacks bestowed,
Insight gained on this path I strode.

Feast of the Mind's Awakening

A feast of flavor spreads so wide,
Where chips and salsa sit with pride.
Each mouthful brings a thoughtful cheer,
As nachos whisper, "Come, draw near!"

Cookie crumbs and sodas fizz,
In joyful treats, the wisdom is.
Each sugary pick twirls in delight,
Bringing laughter deep into the night.

Pretzel twists and candy floss,
Teach me not to count the cost.
For every snack that hits the plate,
Unwraps the secrets of our fate.

So raise your forks and toast the fun,
With every bite, another pun.
For in this feast, our minds engage,
As flavor sparks the perfect page.

Mindful Morsels

A tiny treat, a moment's bliss,
Each morsel whispers, 'You can't miss!'
With cookies soft and doughnuts bright,
Mindful munching feels just right.

A sprinkle here, a drizzle there,
Flavors lift me high in air.
Crunchy bites of wisdom served,
Through every snack, my soul's preserved.

Snacktime giggles, laughter loud,
Awakening thoughts, I feel so proud.
Chocolate bars and crispy rice,
Bring insights wrapped in sugar's slice.

So savor each delight with glee,
For mindful munching sets me free.
In every cheery, tasty dance,
I find the joy in each sweet chance.

Snacks of Self-Discovery

Crunchy chips in hand, oh what a thrill,
Each bite a lesson, each crunch a skill.
Dip into wisdom, guacamole bright,
Snacking on truths, feels just right.

Chocolate whispers secrets, sweet and deep,
In silky wrappers, dreams begin to leap.
Popcorn pops loud, thoughts hover like birds,
Between buttery bites, no need for words.

Gummy bears giggle, as laughter resounds,
With every chew, enlightenment abounds.
The cookie crumbles, but joy sticks around,
In this flavorful journey, happiness is found.

Final sip of soda, a fizzing surprise,
Insights bubbles up, as my spirit flies.
Snack by snack, I stumble, I learn,
In this banquet of life, I happily turn.

Forks of Fortune

With a fork in hand, I navigate fate,
Salads of choices pile high on my plate.
Twirling spaghetti, a noodle of bliss,
Every twist tangles, can't help but reminisce.

The pancake stack teeters, sugary high,
Each syrupy drizzle makes the spirit fly.
Potato wedges whisper, 'You can't be shy,'
With each crispy bite, let your worries die.

Broccoli florets nod in sage approval,
In this feast of fortune, I'm an achiever.
Each slice of pie is a portion of fate,
Savoring life as I laugh and plate.

In this forkful journey, I dance and cheer,
Fortune favors those who munch without fear.
So raise your forks high, let us all rejoice,
In the meal of existence, let's find our voice!

Munchies for Mind Expansion

Nibbles of knowledge, I munch and chew,
With each little snack, my mind breaks through.
Pretzel twists thoughts, all knotted and fun,
A sprinkle of cheese makes the idea run.

Popcorn kernels pop like ideas in flight,
Each fluffy piece feels so wonderfully right.
Candy corn visions, sweet bursts of gold,
With fruity gummies, new stories are told.

Cheesy puffs brighten up cloudy concepts,
While crunchy granola gives wisdom great steps.
A scoop of ice cream chills down my woes,
In this mad munchie feast, my spirit glows.

Final bite of brownie, rich and divine,
Each chocolatey morsel, a thought intertwined.
Munching through life, I giggle and prance,
These snacks of creation give dreams a chance.

Savoring the Journey

As I travel along, each snack tells a tale,
From salty to sweet, I happily sail.
Trail mix of moments, a colorful blend,
Each bite a memory, a joyful friend.

Granola bars strengthen, with crunch and with chew,
Fuel for the soul, each flavor rings true.
With chocolate chips twinkling, like stars up above,
Savoring the journey, I feast on the love.

Cookies fresh-baked, with warmth in each crumb,
Remind me of laughter, remind me of fun.
A whiff of cinnamon swirls in the air,
Each scent beckons stories, I stop and stare.

With every treat shared, connections I find,
In this savory adventure, all hearts intertwined.
The journey is richer with snacks on the way,
Together we munch, come what may!

Nibbles of Nirvana

In a world of chips and pretzels tight,
The quest for wisdom feels just right.
Popcorn wisdom, crispy and light,
Snack on enlightenment, what a delight!

With each crunchy bite, we start to see,
The truth in salsa, pure jubilee.
Each dip a thought, oh can it be?
The nacho path to harmony!

Munching away on thoughts so profound,
Potato chips whisper, wisdom unbound.
In every flavor, there's joy to be found,
Nibbles of bliss, where laughs are renowned!

So grab your treats, let the munching start,
Crackers and cheese, oh what a smart art!
Snack time is sacred, a joyous part,
Crunching into truth is the ultimate heart!

Banquets of Being

Gather 'round the table, snacks to share,
Cookies and laughter fill the air.
Each cheesy grin, a moment rare,
Life's banquet of joy has more than a flair.

Doughnuts of wisdom, sweet delight,
Sprinkles of laughter, oh what a sight!
Each bite a giggle, floating so light,
A banquet of fun, draped in the night.

With popcorn in hand, we ponder the stars,
Crispy debates on life's little jars.
As cakes tell tales of coming afar,
Snack at this feast, and raise the bar!

Eating our way through each little truth,
Banquets of being, the joy of youth.
With cookies and friends, it's no sleuth,
Every crumb a memory, sweet and uncouth!

Appetizing Aha Moments

Oh, the joy of snacks, how they spark,
With each tasty treat, we leave our mark.
A cookie here, a brownie there,
Aha moments bloom, in this feast we share!

Chips crunch like thoughts in our head,
Each bite a revelation, softly said.
When chocolate calls, who can turn red?
Appetizing truths lie where crumbs are spread!

Nibbles of cake and sips of sweet tea,
In bites of bliss, we find the key.
Snack on the silly, oh can't you see?
Each little moment shapes you and me!

So gather your munchies, take a seat,
Share in the flavors, oh what a feat!
For in every snack, wisdom's discreet,
Aha moments served on a platter of sweet!

Comfort from Crumbs

As cookies crumble, hearts start to mend,
Snacks and giggles, the perfect blend.
Bite-size joy, that we all commend,
Crumbs of comfort, around the bend.

With each little morsel, happiness grows,
Potato skins holding secrets nobody knows.
In chocolatey laughter, our spirit flows,
Comfort found in bites, as wisdom shows.

Soft pretzels twist our worries away,
Snacking in bliss, come what may.
With dips and chips, we joyfully play,
Crumbs leading the way, in a bright array!

So here's to the snacks, our sturdy ground,
In laughter and flavor, truth is found.
With crumbs of joy, let's gather around,
The comforts of life, deliciously profound!

Light Snacks, Heavy Thoughts

Chips and dips in hand, I sit,
Contemplating life, in crumbs I'm fit.
A donut here, a pretzel there,
Wisdom's found in cheesy flair.

Peanuts pop in bubbling glee,
Yogurt dips sing songs of spree.
Reality's weight, but snacks so light,
Munching through depth, till full moonlight.

Chewy chocolates take the stage,
A sweet reprieve from life's new age.
Each bite a step, each crunch a thought,
Snack break bliss, a calming plot.

Tantalizing Traditions

Gather round for tasty tales,
Churros dance and laughter wails.
A picnic spread of grand delight,
As wisdom simmered, snacks take flight.

Sushi rolls wrapped up so tight,
Sipping tea, oh what a sight.
Traditions served on plates of fun,
Slurping noodles, we're all one.

Baklava dreams with honeyed threads,
In every crumb, a thought embeds.
With every bite, old stories thrive,
In snack-filled joy, we come alive.

Gourmet Gains

Pasta hills and salad fields,
Life's gourmet offerings, nature yields.
Each morsel brings a thought divine,
A feast of flavors, nothing's benign.

Truffle fries in laughter drown,
Gastronomic dreams spun all around.
With every fork, the mind expands,
Cheesecake thoughts that life commands.

Sauciest ideas, in bubbles rise,
Tasting life, to our surprise.
Through rich delights, we gain our ground,
In every snack, wisdom is found.

Mindful Munching

Crunching carrots with mindful grace,
Every bite, finds its place.
In celery sticks, reflections grow,
As peanut butter thoughts start to flow.

Popping popcorn, kernels dance,
Awareness rises, a tasty chance.
With every nibble, worries fade,
Snack and ponder, happiness made.

Savor each flavor, oh what a thrill,
Tasty tidbits quiet the mind's will.
In every crunch, insight ignites,
Munching mindful with pure delights.

www.ingramcontent.com/pod-product-compliance
Lightning Source LLC
Chambersburg PA
CBHW051701160426
43209CB00004B/974